Kids' Travel Guide
Australia

FlyingKids® Presents:
Kids' Travel Guide
Australia

Author: Angie Droulias

Editor: Carma Graber

Graphic designer: Neboysha Dolovacki

Cover Illustrations and design: Francesca Guido

Published by FlyingKids® Limited

Visit us @ www.theflyingkids.com

Contact us: leonardo@theflyingkids.com

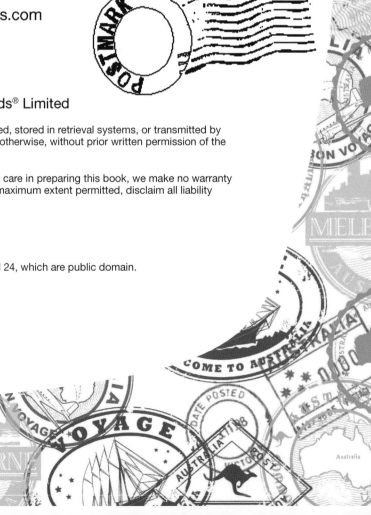

ISBN: 978-1-910994-54-2

Acknowledgments:

All images are Shutterstock, except those on pages 20, 23. and 24, which are public domain.

Table of Contents

This is the only page for parents in this book … 😉

Dear Parents,

If you bought this book, you're probably planning a family trip with your kids. You are spending a lot of time and money in the hopes that this family vacation will be pleasant and fun. You would like your children to learn a little about the country you visit—its geography, history, unique culture, traditions, and more. And you hope they will always remember the trip as a very special experience.

The reality is often quite different. Parents find themselves frustrated as they struggle to convince their kids to join a tour or visit a landmark, while the kids just want to stay in and watch TV. On the road, the children are glued to their mobile devices instead of enjoying the new sights and scenery—or they complain and constantly ask, "When are we going to get there?" Many parents are disappointed after they return home and discover that their kids don't remember much about the trip and the new things they learned.

That's exactly why *Kids' Travel Guide — Australia* was created.

How does it work?

A family trip is fun. But difficulties can arise when children are not in their natural environment. *Kids' Travel Guide — Australia* takes this into account and supports children as they get ready for the trip, visit new places, learn new things, and finally, return home.

Kids' Travel Guide — Australia does this by helping children to prepare for the trip and know what to expect. During the trip, kids will read relevant facts about Australia and get advice on how to adapt to new situations. The kids will meet Leonardo—their tour guide. Leonardo encourages them to experiment, explore, and be more involved in the family's activities—as well as to learn new information and make memories throughout the trip.

Kids' Travel Guide — Australia includes puzzles, tasks to complete, useful tips, and other recommendations along the way. In addition, kids are asked to document and write about their experiences during the trip, so that when you return home, they will have a memoir that will be fun to look at and reread again and again.

Kids' Travel Guide — Australia offers general information about Australia, so it is useful regardless of the city or part of the country you plan to visit. It includes basic geography; flag, symbols, and coins; basic history; and colorful facts about culture and customs in Australia.

Ready for a new experience?
Have a nice trip and have fun!

Hi, Kids!

If you are reading this book, it means you are lucky—you are going to **Australia**!

You probably already know what areas you will visit, and you may have noticed that your parents are getting ready for the journey. They have bought travel guides, looked for information on the Internet, and **printed pages** of information. They are talking to friends and people who have already visited **Australia**, in order to learn about it and know what to do, where to go, and when ... But this is not just another guidebook for your parents.

THIS BOOK IS FOR YOU ONLY—THE YOUNG TRAVELER.

So what is this book all about?

First and foremost, meet **Leonardo**, your very own personal guide on this trip. Leonardo has visited many places around the world (guess how he got there 😉), and he will be with you throughout the **book** and the trip. **Leonardo** will tell you all about the places you will visit—it is always good to learn a little bit about the country and its history beforehand. He will provide many ideas, quizzes, tips, and other surprises. **Leonardo** will accompany you while you are packing and leaving home. He will stay in the hotel with you (don't worry, it does not cost more money 😉)! And he will see the sights with you until you return home.

A Travel Diary – The Beginning!
Going to Australia!!!

How did you get to Australia?

By plane / ship / car / other _____

We will stay in Australia for _____ days.

Is this your first visit ? yes / no

Where will you sleep? In a hotel / In a hostel / In a campsite /

In an apartment / With family / Other _____

What places are you planning to visit?

_____

_____

_____

What special activities are you planning to do?

_____

_____

_____

Are you excited about the trip?
This is an excitement indicator. Ask your family members how excited they are (from "not at all" up to "very, very much"), and mark each of their answers on the indicator. Leonardo has already marked the level of his excitement …

very,
very much

not at all

Leonardo

Who is traveling?

Write down the names of the family members traveling with you and their answers to the questions.

Paste a picture of your family.

Name: _____

Age: _____

Have you visited Australia before? yes / no

What is the most exciting thing about your upcoming trip?

_____
_____
_____

Name: _____

Age: _____

Have you visited Australia before? yes / no

What is the most exciting thing about your upcoming trip?

_____
_____

Name: _____

Age: _____

Have you visited Australia before? yes / no

What is the most exciting thing about your upcoming trip?

_____
_____

Name: _____

Age: _____

Have you visited Australia before? yes / no

What is the most exciting thing about your upcoming trip?

_____
_____

Name: _____

Age: _____

Have you visited Australia before? yes / no

What is the most exciting thing about your upcoming trip?

_____
_____

Preparations at home – DO NOT FORGET ...!

Mom or Dad will take care of packing clothes (how many pairs of pants, which comb to take ...). Leonardo will only tell you the stuff he thinks you might want to bring along on your trip to Australia.

Leonardo made a Packing List for you. Check off each item as you pack it!

☐ *Kids' Travel Guide — **Australia**—*of course 😉
☐ Comfortable walking shoes
☐ A raincoat or umbrella (Sometimes it rains without warning.)
☐ A hat (and sunglasses, if you want)
☐ Pens and pencils
☐ Crayons and markers (It is always nice to color and paint.)
☐ A notebook or writing pad (You can use it for games or writing, or to draw or doodle in when you're bored ...)
☐ A book to read
☐ Your smartphone/tablet or camera
☐ Chewing gum for takeoff and landing

Welcome to Australia—
the most unique land on earth!

Australia is a very special and unusual country. It looks like a huge island in the middle of the ocean—and it has wonderful **beaches**, **mountains**, rainforests, and even a huge **desert** in the center of it!

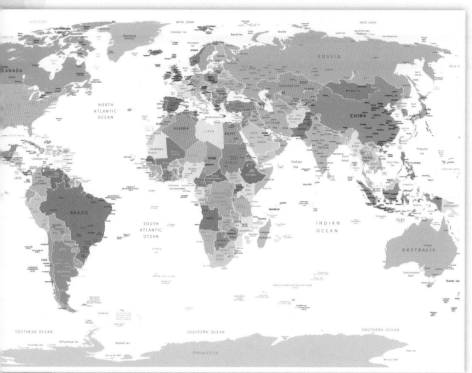

Australia is quite far from the rest of the world, but **over three million travelers** visit the country each year. 😲

Australia was once called "New Holland." It then became known as "Terra Australis," and finally, "Australia."

Leonardo has so much to tell you about this amazing country, so let's get started!

Did you know?
Australia is not just a country—it's also a **continent**! The continent is made up of the mainland, the island of Tasmania, and several smaller islands.

Terra Australis means "southern island." That's because when it was discovered, Australia was the most southern point on the map people used at that time.

Did you know?
Here's something weird: While Australia is technically an island, **you should not compare it to other islands** because it is a continent. If we could compare it with other islands, it would be the largest island in the world!

Australia on the map ... What a shape!

Australia is located in the south on our globe (known as the southern hemisphere). It rests right between two oceans: the **Indian** and the Pacific. The country is more than 7.6 million square kilometers (3 million square miles) wide! Its coastline is almost **26,000 kilometers** 16,155 miles) long.

Look at Australia's shape on the map. Isn't it funny?

Some people think Australia looks a bit like Scooby Doo! What do you think? What does the map of Australia look like to you? Trace the map to come up with ideas!

Australia's states and territories

Australia is made up of six states and two mainland territories. Put an "**S**" for the areas that are states and a "**T**" for the territories below:

__ New South Wales
__ Victoria
__ Northern Territory
__ Queensland
__ Western Australia
__ Australian Capital Territory (ACT)
__ South Australia
__ Tasmania

What is a compass rose?

A compass rose is a design that shows the directions:
North – South – East – West. Since North is always marked on maps, you can always figure out where the other directions are.
A compass rose is drawn on the face of a compass, and the hand always points North. When you know where each direction is, it is easier to figure out where you are … and how to get to where you want to be.

Help Leonardo write down the three missing directions in the blank boxes.

North

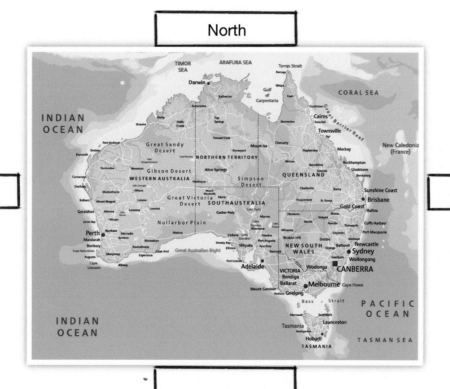

Can you name the seas and oceans that border each part of Australia?

North: _____ Sea and the _____ Sea.

East: _____ Sea, _____ Sea, and the _____ Ocean.

South: _____ Strait, the _____ Australian _____,

and the _____ Ocean.

West: _____ Ocean.

Australia's borders

Borders were invented to separate countries from each other. A border is a line that marks the end of one country's territory and the beginning of another. There are all kinds of borders: sometimes a river or a range of mountains makes a natural border—and sometimes a fence or a special gate marks a border. Other times, borders are only marked by a sign.

Australia's borders are natural borders that are mostly made up of … **ocean water!**

Can you find the two oceans that border Australia by changing the letters around?

dinlna = _____

caPifci = _____

Did you know?
Not one single country actually touches Australia's borders, but there are a few countries that neighbor Australia from the sea.

Quizzes!

Can you find Australia's neighboring countries in the word search puzzle?

- ☐ New Zealand
- ☐ Indonesia
- ☐ Papua New Guinea
- ☐ New Caledonia
- ☐ Fiji

N	B	W	M	J	L	D	R	X	R	F	F	L	Z
D	N	A	L	A	E	Z	W	E	N	M	I	A	S
N	E	W	C	A	L	E	D	O	N	I	A	J	N
K	X	F	Q	I	L	E	G	Y	J	D	P	W	I
C	Q	F	P	E	W	J	Z	D	Z	D	T	S	U
L	R	V	B	U	J	Q	L	R	X	W	G	T	K
A	E	N	I	U	G	W	E	N	A	U	P	A	P
J	C	U	X	A	W	O	N	P	D	Z	U	L	P
P	K	T	U	G	Z	N	D	E	H	O	J	A	R
Z	S	K	I	N	D	O	N	E	S	I	A	O	M

TIMOR SEA

Darwi

Kunur

Halls Creek

andy rt

Lake Mackay

Desert

TRALIA

Great Vic Deser

arbor Pla

Madura

Great Austra

WESTERN AUSTRALIA

QUEENSLAND

Australia's capital: Canberra

Australia's capital city is **Canberra**. Sometimes people call it the "Bush Capital" instead. That's because it's located among forests and farmland. Isn't that a strange place for a capital city?

With less than 400,000 people, Canberra is a pretty small city. But it does have lots of interesting places to see, including the Parliament House, the Telstra Tower, the National Gallery, Commonwealth Park, the National Botanical Gardens, and a fun **kids' museum** called Questacon!

Did you know?
Canberra is situated in the Australian Capital Territory (ACT). It is Australia's smallest territory. It only includes Canberra and the local area around it!

Quizzes!

Do you remember that Australia is made up of states and territories? Have you memorized any? Without looking back, try circling the eight correct ones. Hint: you can check back to page 10.

New Wales   Australian Capital Territory   Northern Territory

Victoria   Queen's Land   Sydney   New South Wales   Perth

South Australia   Tasmania   East Australia   Darwin

Adelaide   Queensland   Western Australia

Australia's major cities:
Stylish Sydney

Sydney is one of the most famous cities in Australia. Nearly **five million people** live in this beautiful city. It's on the east coast of Australia in New South Wales.

Sydney is well-known for its spectacular Opera House, which you may have seen in pictures or postcards. Many concerts, plays, and other big events are held at the Opera House each year. You'll find it near the largest natural harbor in the world, Sydney Harbor (which is also known as **Port Jackson**).

Love Surfing?
Bondi Beach is another popular place in Sydney. It's one of Australia's most beautiful beaches, and it's a top choice for surfers. Even if you're not a surfer, you can enjoy watching the surfers ride the waves! The beach is protected by an underwater shark net—but don't worry, it's a very safe beach!

Did you know?
Sydney has possibly the best weather in Australia. Summers are warm and winters are mild, with no surprises except rain.

 Tip! Take an umbrella and a small surfboard with you to Sydney!

Cultural Melbourne

Melbourne, in the state of **Victoria**, is the biggest Australian city after Sydney. It has four and a half million people. It's famous for its many art galleries and exhibitions—and it's also a lot of fun!

Want to see penguins?
You can see penguins, seals, whales, dolphins, and other animals living in the wild in Port Phillip Bay, and also on a small island called Phillip Island!

Here are the things Leonardo most recommends you do in Melbourne. Check off the ones you did!

☐ Visit the modern city centre and Flinders Street Station.
☐ Take a ride on the Melbourne Star or Puffing Billy Train.
☐ Visit the Melbourne Zoo or Royal Botanic Gardens.
☐ Have a blast at St Kilda's Luna Park.
☐ Travel to the breathtaking Great Ocean Road.

Melbourne has quite a few interesting museums too, such as the Melbourne Museum, the Sea Life Aquarium, the National Gallery of Victoria, and even a real historical prison known as the Old Melbourne Gaol!

Can you see the **Yarra River**? It runs through Melbourne and is 242 km (150 miles) long! Try tracing its shape with a marker or crayon:

Fun Brisbane

Brisbane is one of Australia's sunniest cities. It is the capital of the state of Queensland, which is known for its stunning Gold Coast and Great Barrier Reef.

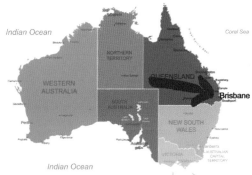

Quizzes!

The population of Brisbane is a little over two million, making it the third largest Australian city. Do you remember which two cities have more people?

A hint: you can find the answer on pages 15 and 16.

In Brisbane, you can visit these popular sights:
- ☐ Story Bridge, which you can climb to reach 80 meters above sea level!
- ☐ The Brisbane Wheel, which looks over the Brisbane River and offers amazing city views.
- ☐ The Museum of Brisbane, where you can marvel at the exhibits or attend a children's workshop.

Want to explore the animals and wildlife? Leonardo recommends you visit the **Lone Pine Koala Sanctuary**, the City Botanic Gardens, and the various parklands found throughout Queensland.

Remember Bondi Beach in Sydney? Not too far from Brisbane, you can find another popular surfing area called Surfer's Paradise. It's located on the famous Gold Coast.

 Brisbane can get very hot during the summer, so make sure to bring light and airy clothes with you—and don't forget your swimsuit!

Sunny Perth

Perth is the capital of Western Australia, the biggest state in Australia. Look at it on the map to see just how big it is!

Perth is set on the Swan River, named for its native black swans. But if you can't find any swans on Swan River, you might want to visit **Lake Monger**, just outside Perth. You are sure to catch a glimpse of these beautiful birds there.

Perth may not be as popular as Sydney or Melbourne, but there are plenty of things to do and places to visit. Mark the ones you visited:

☐ Perth Zoo
☐ The Aquarium of Western Australia
☐ Scitech (planetarium)
☐ Yanchep National Park
☐ Adventure World
☐ Hillarys Boat Harbour for whale-watching!

Did you know?
Perth is one of Australia's **most remote cities**! The nearest big city is Adelaide—over 2,000 kilometers (more than 1,200 miles) away.

Did you know?
Perth is located in one of the driest parts of Australia. Perth averages eight hours of sunshine a day, which is even more than Brisbane!

Flags, symbols, and coins

This is the flag of Australia. It is made up of white stars, a blue background, and a well-known symbol in its top left corner. Do you like it?

But what do the colors stand for?

The colors of the flag represent the following:

Blue – Truth, justice, and loyalty

White – Peace and honesty

Red – Bravery and strength

The main symbols on the Australian flag are called the **Southern Cross**, the **Commonwealth Star**, and the **Union Jack**.

Leonardo needs help figuring out the name of each symbol on the flag. Can you help him by writing the correct number after each name?

The Commonwealth Star _____

The Southern Cross _____

The Union Jack _____

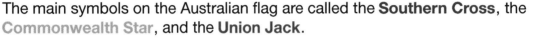

Did you know?
The Commonwealth Star (also called the Federation Star) once had six points, which stood for the six colonized territories of Australia. A seventh point was added to the star almost 100 years later!

Did you match the images to the right names?
Here's what each symbol means:

The **Union Jack** is the flag of the United Kingdom. It's on the Australian flag to show Australia's history as a British colony.

The **Commonwealth Star** features seven points—one point for each of the six Australian states, and one point for the territories.

And lastly, the **Southern Cross** is a real constellation that looks like a small cross. It represents Australia's location in the far south of the world.

All about money ...

How to buy things in Australia!

The official currency (money) of Australia is the **Australian dollar**. One-hundred Australian cents make one Australian dollar.
In order to buy or sell anything in Australia, you will have to use dollars or cents.

Australia's coins look a little like British coins because on the "heads" side, they both show Queen Elizabeth II of England. Here's a picture of Australian coins:

On the other hand, Australia's paper money is probably very different from any other money you have seen! That's because it's not made of paper at all, but of a special kind of **plastic** that doesn't tear!

Heads or Tails!

Leonardo told you that Queen Elizabeth II is on the "heads" side of Australian coins, but what is on the "tails" side? What do all the images on the tails side have in common?

Answer: They are all Australian animals.

Did you know?

There are many more places outside Australia that use the Australian dollar. Those are Christmas Island, Cocos Islands, Heard Island and McDonald Islands, Kiribati, Nauru, Norfolk Island, and Tuvalu.

Australia's history ...
The discovery of Australia

Australia is a very old continent—it dates back to millions of years ago. And while Australia had its own natives living there for centuries, more people came to live in Australia in the 18th century. These settlers came mostly from England, and they created their own colonies in Australia.

Tasman's Discovery
Australia was already known to the Europeans even before the settlers came. That's because Australia was first discovered in **1606** by a Dutch explorer called Abel Tasman. He was the first to call Australia *Terra Australis*.

But Tasman did not settle in Australia, and neither did anyone else until 1770. That's when **Captain James Cook**, aboard his ship *HMS Endeavour*, arrived on the shores of Botany Bay near Sydney.

What is a colony?
A colony is a community created by people who come from another country.

Quizzes!
So who discovered Australia first?

a. Abel Tasman
b. James Cook
c. European settlers

Answer: a. Abel Tasman

Australia's history ...
Meet the Aborigines

Native people lived in Australia thousands of years before the English settled there. The English called these natives "Aborigines." Leonardo wants to tell you more about these people, their culture, and their habits.

Hunting and boomerangs

Aborigines were skilled hunters and fishermen who lived in wild nature. For many years, they used boomerangs to kill animals for food. Today, boomerangs are simply used for fun. Have you ever used a boomerang?

Aboriginal art

Aborigines love art and music, and they have their own special style for each. The picture on your right and the boomerang above show the typical style for Aboriginal painting. Aboriginal artists today still practice this form of painting, which uses mainly dots.

Did you know?
The boomerangs the Aborigines used didn't come back to the thrower. Only the modern ones do!

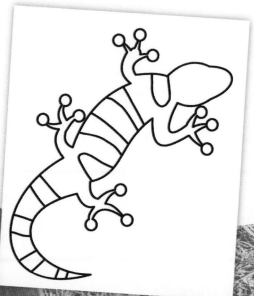

Can you color the lizard using only dots? Make sure to experiment with colors!

The Dreaming ... How the world began?

Aborigines have very special customs and beliefs. They particularly love telling stories, dancing, and singing songs about how they believe the world was created. This creation story is known as the Dreaming or Dreamtime.

What is the Dreaming?

Aborigines believed that their ancestors were the animals of the Earth, and that these animals helped create the world and everything in it. The Dreaming begins with the Spirit of All Life, who dreamt about the world being created and passed the dream on to Barramundi, Currikee, Bogai, Bunjil, Coonerang, and Kangaroo. When Kangaroo passed the dream on to Man, the creation was complete.

Quizzes!

Leonardo is still scratching his head ... Who is Bogai? Currikee? Barramundi? They are all **Aboriginal names for animals** that took part in the Dreaming. Can you guess which animals they are? The pictures below will help you.
Write the correct animal's name below each picture. Number 1 has already been done for you by Leonardo.

1. Kangaroo

Animal: *kangaroo*

2. Bunjil

Animal: _____

3. Barramundi

Animal: _____

4. Currikee

Animal: _____

5. Bogai

Animal: _____

6. Coonerang

Animal: _____

The First Fleet

Leonardo has told you all about how Australia was discovered by the Europeans. Now he'll let you know what happened when the Europeans decided to make Australia their new home. It all began with the First Fleet.

In **1788,** the First Fleet arrived in Port Jackson, Australia. It brought the first European settlers from Portsmouth, England. The fleet consisted of **11 ships** with a total of **1,420 passengers**. Each ship carried soldiers—and also prisoners! The fleet was led by Captain Arthur Philip.

Why prisoners?
Criminals were sent to Australia as part of their punishment, mainly because the prisons in England were full!

Captain Arthur Philip's job was to set up a prisoner settlement in Australia. Between 1788 and 1868, a total of **165,000 convicts** were sent to Australia. In fact, convicts made up most of the population. These criminals were put to work according to their skills. They built bridges, roads, hospitals, and courthouses.

The First Fleet entering Port Jackson on January 26 1788. Creator: E. Le Bihan

Quizzes!

Leonardo needs your help figuring this out. If 780 of the passengers on board the First Fleet were convicts, how many passengers were not convicts?
- **a.** 650
- **b.** 640
- **c.** 698

Answer: b. 640

Meet Ned Kelly—Australia's hero

Leonardo would like to tell you the story of Ned Kelly, Australia's most famous hero. You can call him the "Australian Robin Hood"! He is known for his thick metal armor, which you can see in the picture on the right.

A young hero

Ned was born in **1855** in **Beveridge, Victoria,** but his family was originally from Ireland. Ned was a very brave young man. As a child, he saved another boy from drowning—for which he received a special hero's belt.

The Kelly Gang

Ned Kelly and his gang, known as the Kelly Gang, became very famous in Australia and even England. The members of the gang were his brother Dan Kelly, and their friends Joe Byrne and **Steve Hart**. The Kelly Gang would often get into trouble with the police—but the people loved them and considered them heroes. The police eventually caught up with them, and Ned Kelly was imprisoned and sentenced to death.

Did you know?
Ned Kelly was hung in the Melbourne Gaol. You can visit this old prison, which still stands in Melbourne and is now a museum. You can even visit Ned's cell!

This is what Ned Kelly looked like under the mask!

Quizzes!

Ned Kelly was executed in November 1880. How old was he when he died?

a. 25   b. 15   c. 35

Answer: a. 25

Famous Australians today

Australia is a country known for its culture, entertainment, sports, and adventure. That's why some of the world's most famous actors, **singers**, and athletes are from Australia!

Can you draw a line between the names and what each person is famous for?

Hugh Jackman	Actress
Olivia Newton-John	Rock band
Cathy Freeman	Actor
Russell Crowe	Olympian sprinter
Kylie Minogue	Actor
Ian Thorpe	Actress and singer
Nicole Kidman	Actor
AC/DC	Olympian swimmer
Chris Hemsworth	Singer

Answers: Hugh Jackman – Actor; Olivia Newton-John – Actress and singer; Cathy Freeman – Olympic sprinter; Russell Crowe – Actor; Kylie Minogue – singer; Ian Thorpe – Olympic swimmer; Nicole Kidman – Actress; AC/DC – Rock band; Chris Hemsworth – Actor.

Do you know Australian movies or TV shows ...?
(Hint: see page 30.)

Bon appétit!
Australian food: tasty snacks

Australia is a fairly new country, and its food is quite modern. If you enjoy snacks, baked goods, and fast food rather than traditional meals, you will love Australian food!

The foods described below can be found at nearly all fish 'n' chips shops, which are located in most neighborhoods all over Australia.

Meat pie
First of all, Leonardo recommends you try Australian **meat** pies. They are one of the country's most famous treats. Along with the famed sausage rolls and **chiko rolls**, meat pies are the perfect on-the-go snack. A meat pie is also called a "dog's eye"—but don't worry, there is no dog in this yummy mixture!

Fish 'n' chips
You can't visit Australia without trying some amazing **fish 'n' chips**! Even if you've eaten this delicious meal before, chances are you had a different kind of fish. Australian fish 'n' chips use large pieces of cod, flake, or snapper. They're served with delicious fries—all wrapped in newspaper!

Vegemite
Vegemite is a very famous Australian sandwich spread. It's said that to Australian kids, Vegemite sandwiches are as common as peanut butter and jelly to American kids. But they taste very different! Vegemite is made of yeast extract. It has a **salty taste** that not all people—not even all Australians—are fond of! However, Vegemite is said to be **very healthy**, so be adventurous! Try spreading a little on your morning toast to see whether you like it or not.

Did you know?
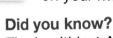
The healthiest Australian snack you can eat, other than Vegemite, is macadamia nuts. Australia supplies the most macadamias in the world—but you'll find they are not cheap!

Australian food: yummy sweets and cakes

Australian food includes lots of delicious sweets and cakes. You can find them at the local supermarket—or even try making them on your own.

Pavlova

A **pavlova** is a very popular Australian dessert made with a meringue. Pavlovas are often decorated with whipped cream and fresh fruits.

Lamingtons

If you like cakes, why not try **lamingtons**? These yummy square sponge cakes contain jam and are coated with chocolate and coconut sprinkles.

Australian biscuits

Australians love their biscuits! If you love chocolate, you should try **tim tams**, but if you want a healthier choice, go for the historical, oat-based **Anzac biscuits**!

Biscuit or cookie? If you live in the United States or some other places, it's a cookie. But in the UK and Australia, it's called a biscuit.

Quizzes!

Which snacks are sweet, and which are savory (salty or spicy)? Mark the pictures below:

Sweet / Savory

Sweet / Savory

Sweet / Savory

Leonardo would like to know your favorite savory dish and your favorite sweet dish from your country! Draw it below and add its name.

My favorite sweet dish:

My favorite savory dish:

Australia is famous for ...
The Great Barrier Reef

One of the most famous sights in Australia is the Great Barrier Reef. It's located in the Coral Sea off the coast of Queensland, and it's extraordinarily beautiful. The Great Barrier Reef is the largest coral reef system in the world—2,300 kilometers (1,430 miles) long! It's made up of 2,900 reefs and 900 islands!

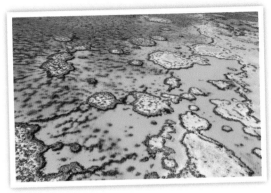

The Great Barrier Reef is home to hundreds of creatures, particularly coral. Over two million tourists visit the Great Barrier Reef every year to admire the marvelous coral and ocean life up close. Leonardo is up for some snorkeling, are you? 😊

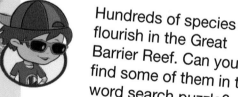

Hundreds of species flourish in the Great Barrier Reef. Can you find some of them in the word search puzzle?

- ☐ Coral
- ☐ Starfish
- ☐ Clams
- ☐ Clown fish
- ☐ Dolphins
- ☐ Whales
- ☐ Stingrays
- ☐ Sea horses
- ☐ Sharks
- ☐ Turtles

S	R	S	E	A	H	O	R	S	E	S	Q
B	E	N	T	P	S	E	L	T	R	U	T
V	M	L	H	Q	I	D	Y	V	S	R	L
T	D	V	A	C	F	O	G	J	K	A	S
S	G	S	Z	H	N	L	T	G	R	Y	L
C	T	Z	L	Q	W	P	O	O	A	Q	M
P	N	A	D	T	O	H	C	R	H	N	P
R	I	P	R	G	L	I	G	L	S	D	J
W	E	J	L	F	C	N	R	B	H	I	C
M	D	S	L	M	I	S	J	O	N	G	Z
C	Z	W	J	T	L	S	C	L	A	M	S
L	G	G	S	X	C	O	H	U	G	Q	P

Australia is famous for ...
The Outback

Look at this vast land in the picture below.
What do you think it is?

This is the huge, dry, remote area in the center of Australia. It actually takes up **two-thirds of the whole country**—or 6.5 million square kilometers (2.5 million square miles)! But less than 60,000 people live there. The name of this area is the Outback.

Is the Outback dangerous?
The Outback can be a dangerous place due to its size and weather. It is very easy to get lost, and you should have a guide with you. You should also have plenty of water and sunscreen. Leonardo wants you to stay safe.

Ayers Rock
The most famous sight in the Outback is **Ayers Rock**. (It's Aborigine name is "Uluru.") This is a giant red rock in the middle of the desert! It is 9.4 kilometers (5.8 miles) around. (That means you would need at least three hours to walk all the way around it!) It is **348 meters (1,142 feet) high**! Would you prefer to climb it or walk around it? 😉

Meet Crocodile Dundee

When people think of Australia and its Outback, a certain person comes to mind: Crocodile Dundee.

A very funny film came out in 1986 that was set in the Outback. The movie, called *Crocodile Dundee*, was about a man who lived barefoot in the wilderness, hunted buffalo, fought with crocodiles, and killed snakes with his bare hands. But it wasn't just a made-up movie: the Crocodile Dundee character was based on a real person—a bushman by the name of **Rod Ansell**.

What is a bushman?
Bushman is an Australian word. It means "a man living in the bush." In Australia, any natural rural area outside the big cities is called the bush.

Rod Ansell

Rod Ansell is known as **"the real Crocodile Dundee."** He became famous all around the world after he survived for 56 days in a remote area with limited supplies. His ordeal began when he decided to go on a fishing trip in 1977—and ended up being stranded on a remote island. He had to hunt every day to feed himself and his two dogs. He also had to work to find fresh drinking water. And he had to protect himself from crocodiles by sleeping in trees with snakes! 😲

Could you survive in the wild? Which five things would you take with you to survive three days in the Outback?

_____ _____

_____

and ... _____

Crocs, sharks, and spiders—oh my!

Australia is known for its unique wildlife. But did you know that some of the most dangerous animals in the world live in Australia? Leonardo would like to warn you about the three you may want to stay clear of: **crocodiles**, **sharks**, and **redback spiders**!

Crocodiles

Crocodiles are found in various rivers and streams in the northern Outback. The most dangerous crocodiles are the Australian saltwater crocodiles. These crocodiles live in both salt water and fresh water—and they can grow up to **7 meters (23 feet) long**!

Sharks

Sharks are also one of the most feared predators in Australia. But you'll only be in danger if you swim out into deep, dangerous waters without taking the right precautions. Over 170 shark species live in Australian waters. The largest sharks can grow up to **6 meters (almost 20 feet) long**!

Redback spiders

And lastly, Australia is home to a particular type of spider called the **redback**. It's named for the color on its back—which is red (or sometimes orange). You can find these spiders practically everywhere, but they prefer to hide in sheltered places like holes, sheds, and storage yards. They are **venomous**, but their bites cannot kill you.

Can you guess which clue describes which animal?

1. Only one person gets attacked by these per year: _____
2. They make very sticky webs: _____
3. They are also called "salties": _____
4. Only the females have big enough fangs to bite: _____
5. The largest of them all is the Great White _____ .

Answers: 1. Sharks; 2. Redback spiders; 3. Saltwater crocodiles; 4. Redback spiders 5. Sharks.

Australia is famous for ...
Its wildlife!

Kangaroos

If you want, you can simply call them "roos," as Australians do! Kangaroos are Australia's most recognized animals. They can be found in all parts of Australia. In some areas, kangaroos can be seen hopping across roads—and even into people's backyards! That's why you may come across Kangaroo signs in certain places.

Did you know?
Kangaroos can't back up—that is, they're unable to walk backward!

Did you know?
A baby kangaroo is called a "joey."

Kangaroos are marsupials (pouched animals) and **macropods** (meaning "big foot"). They have long feet and strong hind legs for hopping long distances. Kangaroos are particularly good at "boxing" with each other. They can jump over 9 meters (30 feet) high!

Quizzes! Thirty feet is how high a kangaroo can jump, but can you guess how far they can jump?

a. 3.7 meters (12 feet)   b. 6 meters (20 feet)   c. 7.6 meters (25 feet)

Answer:
c. 7.6 meters (25 feet)

Cute koalas

Koalas

A **koala** is another animal that lives only in Australia. Sometimes people call them "bears," but that's wrong (even though they do kind of look like teddy bears). Leonardo wants you to know that koalas are actually **marsupials**.

Do you remember what a **marsupial** is? If not, you can look back a page to Kangaroos.

You can find koalas in the east of Australia. They live on trees, especially eucalyptus trees (also known as "gum trees" in Australia). They love chewing on lots of leaves, which they can store in their cheeks and pouches. Koalas may seem pretty lazy—they love relaxing on the trees all day long … 😉

Help Leonardo color the koala!

Did you know? Koalas can sleep up to **18 hours** a day?!

Quizzes!

How much do you think a koala weighs? Remember, they do eat a lot and are quite chubby!

    a. 9 kg (20 lbs.)
    b. 13 kg (30 lbs.)
    c. 4.5 kg (10 lbs.)

Answer:
a. 9 kg (20 lbs.)

Playful platypuses

Platypus

The platypus is one of Australia's strangest animals! It has a duck-like beak, beaver-like tail, and otter-like fur! And to make things even stranger, the platypus is a **mammal**, but it actually lays eggs like a duck would!

Leonardo would like to show you a picture of a real platypus. Isn't it strange?

Platypuses live in small rivers and streams, and they are excellent swimmers. They dive into the water to look for food, and normally they can remain underwater for about **30 seconds**. They prefer to come out at night to feed, and this is why they are considered nocturnal.*

   *Nocturnal is what we call animals that come out mostly at night.

Platypuses can only be found in **eastern parts of Australia**, such as Queensland, New South Wales, Victoria, and Tasmania.

Can you draw a platypus? Give it a name too!

Name: _____

Australia's great
national parks

Australia is full of magnificent national parks. Think **majestic mountains**, **rich rainforests**, and **wonderful waterfalls** and **canyons**! Leonardo suggests you visit some of his favorite national parks listed below.

Karijini National Park

Litchfield National Park

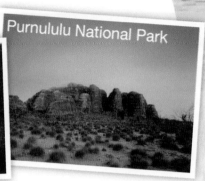
Purnululu National Park

Can you help Leonardo to find the names of the parks in the search puzzle?

- [ ] Kakadu
- [ ] Purnululu
- [ ] Uluru
- [ ] Twelve Apostles
- [ ] Grampians
- [ ] Litchfield
- [ ] Blue Mountains
- [ ] Noosa
- [ ] Carnarvon
- [ ] Karijini
- [ ] Lamington
- [ ] Kalbarri
- [ ] Royal
- [ ] Kangaroo Island

J	Q	G	U	I	S	E	Y	P	N	N	O	Y	L	D
F	G	X	G	D	J	Q	U	M	O	U	K	P	I	N
I	X	J	G	P	A	R	U	C	V	R	A	H	T	A
E	E	T	V	D	N	K	X	U	R	U	R	I	C	L
G	W	K	N	U	V	D	A	X	A	L	I	D	H	S
U	X	U	L	H	G	Z	G	K	N	U	J	U	F	I
A	C	U	R	O	Y	A	L	D	R	Z	I	L	I	O
B	L	U	E	M	O	U	N	T	A	I	N	S	E	O
U	I	R	R	A	B	L	A	K	C	B	I	Q	L	R
O	T	L	W	V	F	S	K	F	G	X	T	D	D	A
S	E	L	T	S	O	P	A	E	V	L	E	W	T	G
Z	Q	F	D	O	X	Y	C	F	X	R	B	C	E	N
L	G	E	N	A	Q	P	P	U	O	J	H	D	R	A
S	N	A	I	P	M	A	R	G	Z	R	H	L	G	K
L	A	M	I	N	G	T	O	N	K	Y	D	K	I	D

Tip!

When you visit a national park, always have water and a small snack with you. Make sure to wear sports shoes or hiking boots.

Talk like an Australian ...

Australians, or "Aussies," may officially speak English, but they sound strange sometimes. That's because of their accents—and some of the funny words they use!

Australian words and phrases

- G'day = hello
- Good onya = well done
- Mate = friend, buddy
- Ace = excellent
- Arvo = afternoon
- Barbie = barbeque
- Chocka = full
- Docket = bill, receipt
- Dunny = toilet
- Exy = expensive
- Mozzie = mosquito

- Ripper = really great, awesome
- Sook = cry, crybaby
- Ta = thanks
- Togs = swimsuit
- Tucker = food
- Servo = gas station
- Stoked = very pleased
- Fair dinkum = really, true
- Too right = definitely
- It's gone walkabout = It's lost—can't be found.

Quizzes!

What is the Australian word for each picture? Fill in the right word underneath.

Can you rewrite these Aussie sentences in your own words? Make sure they have the same meaning.

1. Ta for the barbie—the tucker was ace!

_____

2. I fair dinkum need to use the dunny. Can you stop at a servo?

_____

3. That mozzie bit me through my togs, but now it's gone walkabout!

Fun facts about Australia!

There are so many **fun facts** about Australia. Leonardo wants to tell you a few of his favorites.

It is estimated that humans have lived in Australia for over 45,000 years! 😲

The world's oldest fossil was found in Australia. It is 3.4 billion years old!

In Australia, you'll find more than three times as many sheep as people!

Australia has the world's oldest continually operating roller coaster. It's called "The Great Scenic Railway." You'll find it in Melbourne's St Kilda Luna Park!

Australia has over 750 different types of snakes!

If you visited one new beach in Australia every day, it would take you 29 years to see them all! Can you do the math to find out how many beaches you would have seen in that time?

Answer: In 29 years, you would have visited 10,585 beaches—and there would still be 100 left to see! Australia has 10,685 beaches in all.

More fun facts about
Australia

The Great Barrier Reef has its own mailbox! The mailbox is on the Agincourt Reef. To send a letter with the Great Barrier Reef postmark, you'll need to take a ferry. And remember to use the special Great Barrier Reef stamp!

There is a native Australian bird called the lyrebird. It can copy the calls of over 20 other birds—and even the sounds of cameras and car alarms! 😊

Quizzes! Let's try Leonardo's favorite kind of quiz! Circle TRUE or FALSE for each sentence.

1. No Australian animal has hooves.	TRUE	FALSE
2. The word "selfie" was first coined by Australians.	TRUE	FALSE
3. The largest animal in the world is in Australia.	TRUE	FALSE
4. The Australians invented football, the armored tank (used in war), and the refrigerator.	TRUE	FALSE
5. Australia has three national Frisbee teams.	TRUE	FALSE
6. Fish 'n' chips were first made in Australia.	TRUE	FALSE
7. An Australian train is called a "trainy."	TRUE	FALSE

Answers: 1. TRUE; 2. TRUE; 3. FALSE; 4. TRUE; 5. TRUE; 6. FALSE; 7. FALSE.

Trivia

What do you know about Australia?

Leonardo wants to give you a fun test to see what you've learned about Australia. Are you ready? 😜

1. When was Australia discovered?
   - a. 1770
   - b. 1788
   - c. 1606

2. Which of the following animals is not native to Australia?
   - a. Possum
   - b. Camel
   - c. Dingo

3. Which of the following Australian foods is not sweet?
   - a. Pavlova
   - b. Anzac biscuits
   - c. Vegemite

4. The capital city of New South Wales is:
   - a. Canberra
   - b. Melbourne
   - c. Sydney

5. Which ocean does not border Australia?
   - a. The Atlantic
   - b. The Indian
   - c. The Pacific

6. Which actor isn't Australian?
   - a. Chris Hemsworth
   - b. Sean Bean
   - c. Russell Crowe

7. Where can you find Ayers Rock?
   - a. Uluru
   - b. Purnululu
   - c. Kakadu

8. Which animal lays eggs?
   - a. Kangaroo
   - b. Platypus
   - c. Koala

9. Crocodile Dundee was a(n):
   - a. Animal
   - b. National park
   - c. Movie

10. Which Australian word means "afternoon"?
   - a. Ace
   - b. Arvo
   - c. Servo

Answers:
1=c.; 2=b.; 3=c.; 4=c.; 5=a.; 6=b.; 7=a.;
8=b.; 9=c.; 10=b.

39

And to sum it all up ...

SUMMARY OF THE TRIP

We had great fun! What a pity it is over ...

Which places did we visit?

_____

_____

Whom did we meet ...
- Did you meet tourists from other countries? yes / no
  If you did meet tourists, where did they come from?
  (Name their nationalities):

_____

Shopping and souvenirs ...
- What did you buy on the trip?

_____

_____

- What did you want to buy, but ended up not buying?

_____

Experiences ...
- What are the most memorable experiences of the trip?

_____

_____

_____

What was each family member's favorite place?

_____ : _____

_____ : _____

_____ : _____

_____ : _____

Grade the most beautiful places and the best experiences of your journey:

First place

Second place

Third place

And now, a difficult task—talk with your family and decide:

What did everyone enjoy most on the trip?

A journal

Date   What did we do?

A journal

Date   What did we do?

SURPRISE YOUR KIDS
WITH LEONARDO'S PERSONAL GIFTS!

Every week Leonardo sends prizes (backpacks, posters, stickers, and more) to a few lucky children who read our books. New winners each week!

Just send your email address to enter your child in the drawing. PLUS—each child entered will immediately receive a free Kids' Travel Kit and a 25% off promo code for your next journey with FlyingKids®.

Leonardo wants to make your kids happy!
Sign up today at www.theflyingkids.com/happybuyers

GET A CHANCE TO WIN

ENJOY MORE FUN ADVENTURES WITH LEONARDO AND FlyingKids®

Find more Guides to many destinations at www.theflyingkids.com

Get lots of information about family travel, free activities, and special offers

FlyingKidsForYou   @FlyingKidsForYou   @TheFlyingKids1